Pets From Wood, Field and Stream

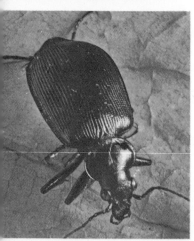

Pets From Wood, Field and Stream

Text and Photographs by Roy Pinney

from *The Golden Book of WILD ANIMAL PETS*

GOLDEN PRESS · NEW YORK

EDITORIAL ADVISORS

JOSETTE FRANK, Director for Children's Books,
Child Study Association of America

DR. LELAND B. JACOBS, Professor of Education,
Teachers College, Columbia University

1969 Edition
Text © copyright 1959 by Western Publishing Company, Inc.
Photographs © copyright 1968, 1959 by Roy Pinney.
Printed in the U.S.A.

CONTENTS

Finding Your Own Pets 7

Caring for Your Pets 15

How To Build a Cage 19

Skunks 27

Raccoons 32

Field Mice 36

Crows 39

Making a Terrarium 43

Turtles 47

Frogs and Toads 53

Salamanders 61

Lizards 64

Insects 67

Health and First Aid 72

Shopping for Pets 76

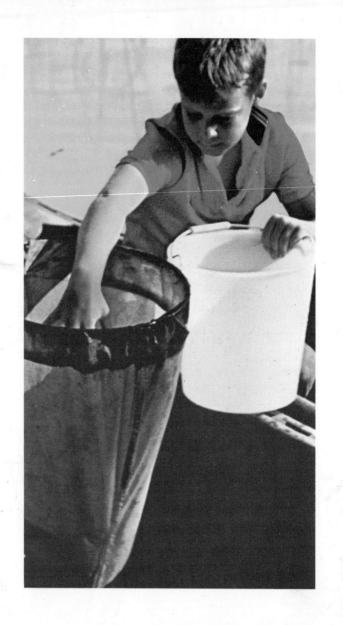

Finding Your Own Pets

THE forests, meadows, lakes, and streams of our country provide homes for a great many forms of animal life. Even the desert has its share of living creatures. The activities of many of the smaller mammals and of most birds, reptiles, and amphibians can easily be observed by anyone who has the patience to sit quietly in one spot. Larger mammals tend to be somewhat shyer, but they also reveal themselves to the patient observer.

Although many animals are active during the day, most of our wildlife creatures are nocturnal by habit. The best time to see them is very early in the morning or late in the afternoon. The experience of seeing these creatures where they normally live is well worth the trouble involved in getting to the right place at the right time.

Another way of becoming acquainted with wild animals is to keep them in your own home or back yard. The animals discussed in this book can be fascinating pets. Almost all of them can learn to respond to you in some degree. A few, such as the raccoon and the descented skunk, can be as good house pets as any dog or cat.

There are several ways to start your own collection of wildlife pets. Most of the animals described in these pages may be purchased through pet dealers. Your local chapter of the ASPCA obtains wild animals from time to time and might give you one if you can prove that you are prepared to care for it properly.

The most thrilling way to get one or more wildlife pets is to capture or trap your own. There is great satisfaction in bringing home some woodland creature and watching it adapt successfully to the new home you have provided for it. This approach has the added advantage of teaching you something about the animal's natural habitat, which you will want to reproduce as closely as possible.

It is a good idea to check with the Conservation Department of your state before you set out on a trapping expedition into the neighboring countryside. Many birds and mammals are protected by law in most states. Some animals may be captured if you obtain a permit, while others may not be trapped under any circumstances.

These laws vary from state to state. There may be no regulation against trapping a particular animal in an area where you and your family are vacationing, but be sure your own state will allow you to take it home.

The equipment you need for your "bring 'em back alive" expedition depends upon the animal you wish to capture. A net and a good-sized bucket will do for most water-

A fine mesh net is perfect for catching frogs.

At low tide, small rock pools by the ocean
are full of aquatic life.

dwelling creatures. If you are collecting
frogs, you will have to keep a top on the
container. Lizards, other woodland reptiles,
and amphibians may also be caught with
a net, or by hand if you are fast enough.

You can carry them home in a covered box or a jar containing moss and leaves.

When you capture any of these cold-blooded creatures, be sure to pick up some of the plants and earth—or water—from the area. This can be used to make their new home very much like their old one.

Mice and raccoons may be captured by means of a so-called live-catch trap. This is simply a baited cage or box which closes as soon as the animal takes the bait. A well-designed trap prevents the animal from being injured.

Your local hardware store is likely to have a variety of traps in different sizes. One that opens at both ends is particularly effective, but be sure it is large enough for the animal you want to attract. In this type of trap the bait must be in the middle to avoid the danger that the trap door may come down on the animal's tail.

The trap should be baited with food which the animal likes but which is not commonly found in the vicinity. Peanut butter or bacon rind is good bait for field mice. Raccoons are fond of sweet corn and sugar-coated vegetables.

Set the trap in an area where the animal you want is apt to be found. A good spot is on the shady side of a log or stump. Cover the top of the trap with leaves and twigs so that it is not too conspicuous.

Be sure to visit your trap every day, for it is cruel to leave a baited trap unattended. A captured animal will be frightened and, very likely, hungry and thirsty. A trap for a small animal should contain some leaves

The Havahart trap is designed to catch small animals without harming them.

and moss in which it can curl up at night. If the trap seems untouched for two or three days, move it to another position and put in fresh bait.

Avoid handling any newly captured creature. It will not be able to understand what has happened and will probably try to bite you. Leave it in the trap and carry it home as gently as you can. Do not expose it to drafts or direct sunlight.

A trap is not particularly selective in its choice of victim. It will catch any animal that tries to seize the bait. If you find that you have caught a chipmunk or squirrel, it is advisable to release it, as they do not make good pets.

Before you add any wild mammal to an already existing collection, take it to a veterinarian for an examination and possibly an anti-rabies shot. In this way you can be sure that the animal is not diseased. Wild rodents are particularly susceptible to lice and other parasites. Treatment is described in the chapter on Health and First Aid. You can examine cold-blooded creatures, yourself, for any unusual condition.

Caring for Your Pets

OWNERSHIP of any pet entails responsibility as well as pleasure. This applies to both domestic and wildlife pets, but there are some special problems in dealing with wild animals.

The instincts which made it possible for your pet to survive in the rugged world of Nature are quite useless in protected surroundings. You must provide it with food, a comfortable climate and surroundings, and, in many cases, affection and attention.

Small creatures kept in cages and terrariums must be provided with a home as much as possible like that in which they usually live. If you set up their surroundings properly, these pets often do better in captivity than in the wild, for they are protected from their natural enemies.

Cleanliness is also an important part of your responsibility. Cages must be cleaned regularly, and terrariums must be kept free of foul water and mildew.

Despite all your precautions, animals do occasionally injure themselves or become

A pet depends entirely upon you for its food.

sick. This requires immediate attention. You will find this subject discussed on page 72.

Most mammals require more than mere attention to their physical needs. Mice, for instance, are unhappy without companionship. Without at least one other of their kind, these creatures would soon perish of loneliness.

Larger mammals adjust fairly easily to a solitary life, but they do require the companionship of their owners. Raccoons and skunks are naturally playful. A daily play period is essential to their health and well-being. The response of any of these animals to affection and gentle handling is a most rewarding experience.

As an animal-keeper, you have responsibilities not only to your pets but also to your friends and neighbors. You and your family may find the mischievous antics of a pet crow or raccoon quite amusing. You must not expect the family next door to feel the same way if their garden is uprooted or a piece of jewelry is stolen. Unfortunately, you cannot train your pets to respect property rights. The only solution is to keep them away from places where they can get into trouble.

You must also be careful about letting friends handle wildlife pets. It is a good idea to politely but firmly forbid any inexperienced person to pick up an animal. A creature which seems completely tame may react angrily to an unfamiliar and inexpert touch. Your family is legally responsible for any injury to another person. You also, of course, want to avoid injury to your animals.

If you leave your house for a day or more, you must arrange to have your pets provided for. Make sure that the person who agrees to look after them knows what and when to feed them, and what to do in case of illness. Be sure to pick someone who likes animals.

A newly captured animal that does not seem to adjust to captivity may be released where you found it. But you cannot always do this with a pet that has been with you for a long time, particularly if you have raised it from babyhood. It may no longer be equipped to deal with the problems it is apt to meet in a wild state. If you cannot keep a pet for any reason, always try to find a new home for it. Your local zoo or animal society may help.

To stay happy and healthy, a pet must have attention and affection.

How To Build a Cage

MOST pet shops carry an assortment of animal cages in various shapes and sizes. However, prices are often high and you may have difficulty finding exactly what you want.

The best way to get a cage which is just the right size for the pet you want to keep and the space you have available is to build it yourself. With simple materials, a few basic tools, and a little planning, you can build a cage which will fit all your requirements.

The first thing to do is to determine the type and size cage you need. There are several factors to take into consideration. The cage in which an animal is confined should be at least twice the animal's length and at least twice as high. But this is adequate only if the animal is taken out frequently for exercise. If it is to spend most of its time confined, the cage has to be much larger.

Cages must be cleaned frequently, so design yours to make this job as easy as possible. Every part of the cage should be accessible from the outside. Building materials should be of metal rather than wood, for wood retains moisture and odor and is difficult to clean. Because it resists corrosion, aluminum is the best metal to use.

Safety is another important consideration. Be sure that there will be no sharp wires, rough edges, or pointed objects either inside or outside the cage.

You can make an excellent small cage out of ordinary cake-cooling racks. These racks usually come in nine-inch squares and may be found in any housewares store. They can be put together very much like an erector set, enabling you to design the cage in almost any form you wish.

The easiest tools to work with are hog ring pliers and half-inch rings. The ring pliers cost about three dollars and are a worthwhile investment if you intend to build more than one cage. However, you

Hog ring pliers and rings are used to join together cake-cooling racks.

can use ordinary pliers.

When building the cage, keep the feet of the cooling racks on the outside. They will raise the floor of the cage off the surface on which it sits. One of the side or top racks should be permanently fastened on one side only so that it can be used as a door.

Oven racks can be put together in the same way. They will give you an even sturdier construction.

If you paint your cage, be sure to choose a paint that does not contain lead. Any animal is likely to gnaw the bars of its cage, and lead-base paint is poisonous.

A sheet of metal or a layer of newspaper may be put on the bottom of the cage to make a comfortable floor. Make it small enough to leave a slight border all the way around for ease in cleaning. Be sure, if you use the metal, that the edges are not sharp.

Sometimes, small mice can squeeze through the bars of this kind of cage. In that case, you can keep your mice in a cage of quarter-inch wire mesh.

Burrowing animals such as mice must

have a nesting box into which they can retreat. As a matter of fact, most caged animals seem to appreciate a small box in which they can curl up and hide or go to sleep.

A nesting box is a substitute for an underground burrow or a hole in a tree, so it should not be too roomy. An ordinary cigar box with a hole cut in the side will do for tiny creatures. You can use a shoebox or a similar packing carton for larger animals.

The nesting box should have a door so that you can keep the animals inside while you are cleaning the rest of the cage. The nesting box itself must also be cleaned regularly.

Place the food and water containers so that they can be reached easily from the outside, preferably without opening the door. Make sure that the water cup is attached firmly enough to prevent its being upset by a drinking animal.

If you want to build a large outdoor cage, you will have to work with wire mesh. Fourteen-gauge Permaguard woven wire is a strong material that will last up to ten years if you keep it clean. You can purchase it by the foot or in rolls. A one-inch by two-inch mesh will do for larger animals. You can also make a small cage out of this wire, but you should pick a smaller mesh size.

A wire cutter, the hog ring pliers and half-inch rings should be used to work with the wire mesh. The wire may be bent to form a top and two sides, or you can make a frame out of wood and attach the wire to it with heavy staples. Be sure the door is placed in such a way that you can reach every part of the cage. This is important not only for easy cleaning of the cage, but

A large cage can be made of wire-mesh stapled to a wood frame.

for reaching the animal in case it is sick and refuses to come out.

The bottom of a cage for fur-bearing animals should be covered with a thin layer of sand or cedar shavings. This provides a comfortable floor, and also gives the animals a surface they can use to rub off the excess oil in their coats. This keeps their fur from becoming too dirty and helps to prevent mange.

Fresh sand or shavings should be supplied frequently, preferably every day in a small cage. The old material can be dumped out easily by raising the metal floor and letting the shavings slip through the mesh bottom into a receptacle underneath. Sponge off the flooring thoroughly before you cover it with a new surface.

Cleanliness is extremely important to the well-being of your animals. At least once a week the entire cage must be washed thoroughly mild disinfectant solution. Be sure to remove the animals before you do this, and rinse the cage out well before you put them back. There must be no trace of disinfectant for them to swallow.

Skunks

In its wild state, the skunk is not a very popular creature. But it does not really deserve this bad reputation. The skunk is gentle by nature and uses its powerful weapon only when it thinks it is in danger.

Skunks take readily to domestic life. They are playful, affectionate, and easy to care for. Skunks sold as pets are already descented. This is done by removing two small glands called "musk glands," and means that you don't have to worry about getting an accidental spraying.

A skunk is best obtained through your local pet dealer or from a commercial skunk breeder. Buy one about seven or eight weeks old. At this age it is old enough to be separated from its mother but young enough to begin to respond to training. In addition, removal of the musk glands at the base of the tail is a simple operation with baby skunks, but it can be a serious matter with adult animals.

Even before your pet skunk arrives, you should prepare a place for it to stay. Skunks normally live in burrows, hollow logs, or small rock caves. Your baby skunk will therefore feel safest in a dirt-lined box or a cage with a roof. If you keep your skunk outside, make sure that its home is protected from dampness.

At the beginning, you will have to spend a lot of time caring for your pet. A seven- or eight-week-old skunk must be fed with an eye dropper or a nursing bottle. Like human babies, it needs a milk formula. A mixture of condensed milk, water, and a few drops of Karo syrup will do nicely. Since a baby skunk has only a very small stomach, you should feed it a small amount every few hours.

With good care and gentle handling, your skunk will grow rapidly. Before long it will be able to eat vegetables and scraps of meat. Meat is an important part of its diet since skunks require protein to stay healthy. Cod liver oil and vitamins should also be added occasionally. When fully grown, your skunk will thrive on one good meal a day.

Skunks are quite nearsighted and do not always see their food when it is put down.

A skunk may eat table scraps, but the rest
of its diet must be balanced.

For this reason it is a good idea to develop
some sort of special call or whistle to use
only at feeding time.

Skunks normally hibernate during severe
winters. If you live in the northern part of
the country, your skunk will probably develop a ravenous appetite as winter approaches. Be careful not to overfeed it during this period. If you do, your skunk w

just become fat and sleepy.

If you have the space, it is best to provide your skunk with a permanent home in the back yard. But you can still give it free run of the house. Remember that it can be treated in much the same way as a dog or cat. Skunks can be paper-trained or housebroken, and can be taken for walks on a leash.

If you keep your skunk outside, it is important to see that it has a shady place to stay during the day. Too much exposure to the sun can give it a dangerous burn.

A skunk is a friendly and playful pet.

You will get a lot of pleasure out of your pet skunk. But remember that there are some responsibilities too. Without its musk glands, the skunk has no means of self-protection. It can only run slowly, and it cannot climb trees. If you let it roam freely, you must be sure that it is not in danger of attack from neighboring dogs. And you must never set it free in the woods. A de-scented skunk that is set free is at the mercy of its natural enemies and will surely not survive very long.

A raccoon can be kept outside all year
if its cage is large and it is protected
from the weather.

Raccoons

WITH their mask-like markings around the
eyes and their ringed tails, raccoons are un-
usually handsome animals. They make in-
telligent and amusing pets.

Most raccoons take to domestic life easily.
You will find that you can lead yours about
on a leash and give it considerable freedom

in the house or in the yard. But do not allow it to wander about the house without supervision. Its curiosity is limitless, and it is likely to get into just about every drawer and cupboard. It can do a lot of mischief with its claws unless closely watched.

The best home for your raccoon is an outdoor cage. It should be made of strong wire mesh extending down into the ground at least two feet. This will keep your pet from digging its way out when no one is around.

If you must keep your raccoon indoors,

and its cage is not very large, take it out every day for play and exercise.

An outdoor cage should be placed so as to allow a choice of sunshine or shade. A waterproof canvas top will provide shelter from bad weather. If you can build the cage as high as six feet, put a box house in an upper corner with a ladder leading to it.

Raccoons are easy animals to feed. They like meat of all kinds, fish, fresh-water clams, and corn and other vegetables. Scraps from your table can supply a good part of your pet's diet. The raccoon's main meal should be in the early evening.

One of the raccoon's most charming habits is connected with feeding. If a raccoon has a pan of water nearby, every morsel of food will be carefully washed before it is eaten. This is always an entertaining ritual to watch.

As winter approaches, your raccoon's appetite will increase. Be careful not to overfeed your pet at this time unless you have provided a place for it to hibernate. In snow country particularly, raccoons spend the coldest part of the winter curled up in

Raccoons carefully wash every bit of food
they eat if water is available.

a hollow tree, sometimes with two or three
bunkmates.

Baby raccoons are born in April or May
in litters of from three to six. Their mother
usually takes good care of them. If, however, you find you have to feed a baby
raccoon yourself, start with a bottled formula and gradually work up to solid foods.

A raccoon that has been raised in captivity will probably be very content as a
permanent member of your family. However, if your raccoon is already full-grown
when you get it, it may have difficulty in
adjusting to its new life. A bad-tempered
animal who refuses to eat makes a poor
pet, and is best released.

Deer mouse

Field Mice

FIELD mice inhabit the meadows and forests of our country. The two most common varieties, the white-footed or deer mouse and the slightly smaller meadow mouse, make good pets. They are hardy and active and, unlike their cousin the house mouse, clean and odorless.

Your mouse cage should be equipped with a nesting box and an exercise wheel. Cover the floor of the cage with a thin layer of fine sand. The mice will use this sand to "dry-clean" their fur by rubbing off the excess oil. You must also keep them supplied with twigs or small pieces of wood. All rodents require something to gnaw on, for their teeth grow continually. The twigs help them to keep their teeth from becoming too long.

The "metabolism wheel," as it is called, may be purchased in any pet store. Mice are extremely active and must have a means of exercise. They use the wheel as a treadmill and often keep it going for hours. They will play on ramps and ladders, too.

Field mice are easily caught in a livecatch trap. Use cheese, peanut butter, or oatmeal as bait. As always, remember to

Mice should be kept in a cage with a nesting box and an exercise wheel.

inspect the trap every day, for mice cannot survive very long without food and water.

Feed your mice two meals a day. A varied diet of insects, grain, nuts, and green vegetables is best. Raw meat should be given only occasionally, as too much tends to make mice vicious.

Food and water should be offered in flat, shallow dishes that cannot be overturned easily. You can leave a panful of grain or nuts in the cage all day so that the mice can munch on these delicacies whenever they wish. The rest of their food should be taken away after they have eaten for an hour.

Since the cage must be cleaned every day, it is a good idea to put a door on the nesting box. Then you can lure the mice in there and keep the door closed while you are cleaning.

Female mice are good mothers, but the fathers do not always treat their blind, hairless infants too kindly. For this reason it is a good idea to separate the father from the rest of the family until the babies are old enough to take care of themselves.

Crows

BECAUSE of its intelligence, curiosity, and lack of fear, the crow can be a marvelous pet. A young crow will make itself thoroughly at home in your house. It will probably follow you around, cackling and whistling and demanding attention.

Many adult crows can be tamed easily, but you will have the best chance for success if you get a crow that is quite young.

Your new pet crow will seem to be constantly hungry. Feed it often, but only a little bit at a time. Hold an insect or worm over the crow's head and drop it in when the crow opens its beak. As it gets older, your crow will learn to pick up food from a dish. You can teach a crow to respond to a food call if you repeat the call every day at feeding time.

Young birds ordinarily get all the moisture they need from their food. They never see water until they start to fly, and then they learn to drink by imitating their parents. Because your bird has been deprived of this experience, you will have to teach it how to drink. Offer it a few drops of water from a medicine dropper. Once it accepts this, gently hold its head in a water cup. Before long it will be able to help itself whenever it wants water.

Your crow's cage can be a simple wire enclosure with a sand floor and a wooden perch bar. But no crow should be confined to the cage after it has become accustomed to its new quarters. Leave the door open most of the time to let it come and go. Have a veterinarian clip the ends of the long wing feathers to prevent your crow from flying away. Then it can be allowed to roam around the house and yard, but be sure it is protected from cats, dogs, and other animals.

Given the opportunity, an adult crow can find all the insects it needs around your lawn and garden. This natural diet should be supplemented with raw meat, fruit, and vegetables. Canned dog or cat food can also be used. Clean drinking water should always be available.

Crows like to keep themselves clean. In warm weather your pet will take a daily bath if you provide it with a "bathtub." Any flat-bottomed receptacle will do nicely if the inside is not too slippery. Be sure that it is sturdy enough to bear your crow's weight without tipping. In winter, a small box of clean sand can replace the bathtub. This dry bath will help the crow to stay clean and sleek.

A crow will be interested in everything you do.

Crows will hide anything they can pick up, particularly if it is bright and shiny. If your mother is missing a piece of jewelry, you can be sure that your crow is the culprit. You can usually find the stolen article by keeping a close watch on the thief. Sooner or later it will decide to move its loot to another hiding place and you can catch it with the goods.

Crows are good mimics and can reproduce many different sounds. With patience, you may even be able to teach one to say a few words. Take a simple word such as "hello" and repeat it several times slowly and clearly. Continue the lesson each day until your crow imitates the sound. Once it has learned one word you can start it on another.

It is not true that your crow will learn to talk more quickly if you slit its tongue. This is a cruel practice and will probably prevent the bird from talking at all.

The crow's western relative, the magpie, also makes a good pet. It is strikingly colored and has a long tail. Magpies learn to talk more easily than crows.

Making a Terrarium

WHENEVER possible, zoos and museums exhibit animals in their natural environment. A terrarium allows you to do the same thing on a small scale in your own home. A rectangular glass aquarium is an ideal enclosure for a terrarium.

A miniature, glass-enclosed forest makes a fine home for toads, young box turtles, and some types of salamanders and lizards. An expedition into a wooded area near your home is likely to turn up a number of suitable specimens. Do not put creatures you find along the edges of streams and ponds into a woodland terrarium, for they probably require a semi-aquatic home.

Along with your container, you will need coarse sand, rich soil, and a supply of small bushes, ferns, and rocks. Wash the sand thoroughly and use it to cover the floor of the terrarium to a depth of about two inches. Put an equal amount of soil, or wood loam, on top of the sand.

At this point you can start landscaping. To create different levels, make at least one

little hill. A few rocks and a piece of dead wood can add interest to the display. Now you are ready to plant the ferns and bushes. They should be inserted firmly into the soil and watered thoroughly at the roots. Follow nature's pattern by creating both shady and open areas.

With a final sprinkling of water to saturate the topsoil, your terrarium is ready to receive your pets.

A semi-aquatic terrarium is suitable for

Good landscaping makes a woodland
terrarium interesting.

frogs, turtles, and most salamanders. Materials required are much the same as those used in the woodland terrarium, but you must clearly separate the land and water areas.

A low partition will serve to hold back the sand and loam. Allow the land area to slope down to the water so that it is like the bank of a stream.

Woodland and semi-aquatic terrariums

should both be covered with a glass top to keep in the moisture. If any signs of mildew appear, substitute a screen cover for a few days until the surplus water evaporates.

A dry, sand-covered tank planted with clumps of grass, cactus, and other desert plants makes an ideal home for most lizards and is called a desert terrarium. The sand should be washed and then mixed with charcoal and a small amount of lime. You can obtain the plants you need from a florist.

Use a rubber-bulb sprayer to moisten the base of the plants occasionally, but make sure that the sand is kept dry. The cover of the desert terrarium should be made of wire mesh to allow ventilation.

Terrariums can be of any size, from small fruit jars to huge displays seen in zoos and museums. Whatever the size of your terrarium, be sure to take the time to set it up properly at the beginning. It will then require only a little attention each day. Be sure, also, to build the right type of terrarium for your animals.

Box turtle

Turtles

TURTLES are among the easiest animals to keep as pets. Most of them need little space, and their food requirements are simple. Although they are not particularly active, they are interesting to observe. Many pet turtles have learned to recognize the approach of human beings. Some have even been taught to respond to a food call.

Turtles can be found or bought almost anywhere. They live in and around ponds and streams in all parts of the country.

There are many varieties of turtles. All

47

but a few like to divide their time between land and water. So most turtles will adjust easily to a small semi-aquatic aquarium.

Since turtles are cold-blooded animals, it is important to keep the temperature of their surroundings fairly warm. An ordinary desk lamp can provide enough heat during cold winter nights. It is also advisable to change the water whenever it becomes fouled. Be sure that the fresh water is not too cold.

Turtles enjoy sunning themselves, but they cannot stand direct sunlight for long periods. You must therefore provide a shady area if the terrarium is exposed to the sun.

All aquatic turtles enjoy swimming. You can give them a special treat once in a while by filling up the bathtub and allowing them to swim for an hour.

An ideal place for land turtles is an outdoor enclosure. A fenced-in area measuring about three feet by four feet will give you enough room to keep two or three land turtles. If the ground is hard, cover it with a layer of clean sand. A few firmly anchored plants or bushes will be required for shade.

If there is enough rainfall in your area, you will not have to provide water. However, a panful of water will enable your turtle to soak itself once in a while.

All turtles living in cold climates hibernate during the winter. If you keep land turtles outdoors, make sure that the ground is soft enough for them to dig into, or provide them with a small cave. At the first frost, they will disappear into their winter quarters and not be seen until spring.

In their normal environment, turtles eat

A semi-aquatic terrarium is a good home
for most small turtles.

insects, freshwater clams and mussels, fish, and aquatic greens. The commercial turtle food sold in most pet stores does *not* supply enough nutritive value for them. You should also feed them raw ground meat, bits of fish, and an occasional piece of lettuce or other leafy vegetable.

Baby turtles should be fed a small amount every day, but they can go a day or two without food if necessary. Break the food into small bits for the babies. Older turtles can tear meat and plants to the proper size with their bills and feet. They should be fed only twice a week.

Water-dwelling turtles like to eat under water. Drop their food directly into the water, preferably in front of their noses. When your turtle gets to know you, it may swim over and take its meal from your hand.

A turtle whose shell becomes soft, or whose growth seems slow, is probably suffering from poor diet. Bone meal and cod liver oil mixed with meat usually take care of the trouble. Regular doses of vitamins help to prevent diet deficiency.

It is just as easy to make a pet out of a full-grown turtle as to raise one from a baby. During the spring and summer, adult turtles are hard to catch. They may be sunning themselves lazily on a rock or log, but as soon as you come near they plop into the water. Late in the fall, just before they hibernate, they become more sluggish. It is often possible to sneak up on one then.

The turtle you buy in a pet store is likely to be a baby. Novelty shops sometimes paint the shells of baby turtles. If you get one like this, start removing the paint immediately. It prevents the shell from growing and will eventually injure the turtle. The shell has no nerve endings, so you can chip the paint away with a knife without hurting your turtle. Be careful not to crack the shell and do *not* use solvents!

There are two species of turtles which should never be kept as pets. These are the snapping turtle and the softshell turtle. Both of these species have vicious tempers, and their powerful jaws are capable of inflicting considerable damage to anyone who comes within their reach.

Toad

Frogs and Toads

FROGS and toads, together with salamanders, make up that curious group of
animals known as amphibians. Most frogs
and toads are equally at home in water or
on land. This is also true of some, but not
all, salamanders. The unique characteristic
of all but a few amphibians is that they begin their lives in water. Only after they have
become adults can they climb out onto land.

It is fascinating to watch the change from
egg to tadpole to frog or toad. You can
easily give yourself the chance to observe
this spectacle.

53

Frogs and toads lay their eggs in the spring. To collect some, you need only a glass jar with a few holes punched in the cover. Walk along the edges of any pond or stream until you see a mass of white, jelly-like eggs lying in shallow water. Fill the jar with some water from the stream or pond and then carefully scoop up the eggs.

At home, transfer the eggs to a larger container or a small aquarium. Hatching time varies, depending upon the species and the temperature, but you will have a crop of tadpoles within three to ten days.

Tadpoles need plenty of room to swim around in, even when they are tiny. But do not keep them in the same tank with larger fish or they will probably be eaten. They can be transferred to a community aquarium after a couple of weeks.

Newborn tadpoles live on food stored up in their tails. As they begin to develop, they feed on the algae that grows on underwater rocks. Take some of the mossy rocks from a local stream and transplant them to your home aquarium. This should take care of

Tadpoles can be scooped out of ponds
or streams with a net.

the food supply for your tadpoles. Once in
a while you can also give them some bits of
lettuce, or finely chopped meat.

Sometime during the summer, your tads
will start to develop hind legs. Their tails
will gradually shrink and then front legs
will appear. Before long the change will be
complete and your frogs or toads will be
ready to come out of the aquarium.

Neither frogs nor toads can swim indefi-
nitely, so you will have to provide some
means for them to get out of the water. A
few rocks that rise above the surface will
do. Place the rocks in the aquarium before

The leopard frog is an ideal resident
of the indoor terrarium.

the tadpoles complete their transformation.

When they change you will want to know
whether your pets are frogs or toads. It is
not always easy to tell the difference. As a
rule the toad has a rougher skin and squatter
body than the frog.

The eggs themselves can often give you
a clue as to whether they were laid by frogs
or toads. Frogs' eggs tend to cluster in an
irregular mass, while toads' eggs are usually
strung together like beads.

Most frogs spend a good part of their lives in water. Toads are less dependent on water. Although they return to streams or ponds during the spring mating season, they may be found far away from water at other times of the year. Almost every garden has its share of toads. They usually hide in rock crevices or under piles of moist leaves during the day and come out at night to consume huge quantities of harmful insects.

There is no truth to the story that handling a toad can cause warts. The lumps on a toad's back do contain a sticky substance which is given off when the toad is seized by a larger animal. The fluid is slightly poisonous and irritates the mouth of the attacking animal. However, it has no effect on human skin. The only trouble could come from handling a toad and then rubbing your eye. This can cause some inflammation.

Because of their tremendous appetites, it is hard to keep toads in captivity. Many frogs, however, are easily kept in a terrarium or an outdoor enclosure.

The woodland terrarium is suitable for

all types of infant frogs, but the earth must be kept very moist. Ferns, moss, and damp leaves will make the frogs feel at home. A shallow pan or dish will provide enough water. Even adult frogs generally need no more than two inches of water, but they are more comfortable in a semi-aquatic terrarium.

It takes several years for frogs to mature, so a terrarium will house your pets adequately for quite some time. If your frogs are not too large when they become adults, you may keep them in a terrarium permanently. But do not overcrowd them.

Large frogs are usually better off in an outdoor enclosure. You can fence in any damp, shady area and dig a small pit for water. Wire mesh is good fencing material, but remember that you will also need a top. Frogs are remarkable jumpers and might easily escape if their enclosure is not covered.

All frogs and toads hibernate during the winter, so you must be sure that the ground underneath your frog pool is soft and muddy. When cold weather comes, your frogs will burrow into the mud and stay there until spring. Do not disturb them.

If it is not convenient for you to build an outdoor enclosure, you will probably want to release most of your frogs when they are grown. They can be set free near any body of fresh water. You can always start the cycle all over again by finding a new cluster of eggs in the spring.

Wood frogs are fine inhabitants for woodland terrariums.

It is likely that frogs kept outdoors will find all the food they need among visiting insects. But terrarium-dwelling frogs must be fed by hand. Frogs eat only moving objects, so you cannot simply leave food in a dish and walk away. Use tweezers or a piece of string to dangle an insect or a worm in front of the frog. It will be gone as soon as it attracts the frog's attention.

Frogs eat all kinds of insects and worms. If these are sometimes hard to supply, small pieces of raw meat may be substituted. Frogs should be fed two or three times a week. Remember also that big frogs eat little frogs. If you are keeping a lone bullfrog in a large terrarium, do not put infant frogs in with him, for a few will disappear every night.

Any pet can become accustomed to being picked up, and frogs are no exception. Grasp a frog firmly just above the hind legs. He may try to escape the first few times, but before long he will submit to being picked up without protest. Some frogs will even learn to accept food from your hand while you are holding them.

Spotted salamander

Salamanders

SALAMANDERS are amphibians. They are closely related to frogs and toads and have a similar life cycle. The salamander's eggs are laid in water and hatch out in a tadpole-like larval stage. In time, these water-bound creatures change into their adult form and climb out onto land. Some go through a third stage and return to water permanently.

Salamanders may be recognized by their smooth, and sometimes slippery, skin. Unlike lizards, they do not have scales. They require a considerable amount of moisture and are usually found around the edges of streams or ponds and in moist wooded areas.

You can watch the transformation from egg to adult by following the same procedure described in the chapter on frogs and toads. Salamander eggs are also jelly-like and may be collected in the spring.

The eggs of the spotted salamander are lumped together like frogs' eggs, but may be identified by the dark brown spot in the center of each egg. The newt lays its eggs on the leaves of underwater plants. Each egg is separate. Do not try to remove the eggs from the plant. Instead, carefully dig up the entire plant and carry it home in a bucket of water. It can then be transplanted to your own aquarium. Do not keep fish in the same tank, for they will regard the eggs as an especially desirable delicacy.

The semi-aquatic terrarium is the best place to house most salamanders. If your water area is large enough, you can transfer the tadpoles to the terrarium at a fairly early stage. They can climb onto the land portion when they are ready. If you want to keep frogs in the same enclosure, you will have to provide a shallow bathing place. A few flat rocks next to the "bank" will do.

In the larval stage, salamanders can be fed small bits of liver and the yolk of hard-boiled eggs. As adults, they will eat insects, worms, and pieces of raw meat. Most salamanders are active only at night, but they can often be coaxed into changing their habits if you feed them during the day.

The common newt is the most frequently encountered salamander in the eastern part of the country. It is also one of the easiest to keep in captivity. The normal life of the newt has three stages. The tadpole changes into a reddish creature called an eft, which spends two or three years on land. It then becomes yellowish-green and returns to water, where it develops a broad tail useful in swimming. Black-rimmed red dots mark the sides of both eft and newt. Length ranges from three to four inches.

The spotted salamander prefers to live on land. It can be identified by the large yellow or orange spots on its black back. It reaches a length of about seven inches and makes a good resident of the woodland terrarium.

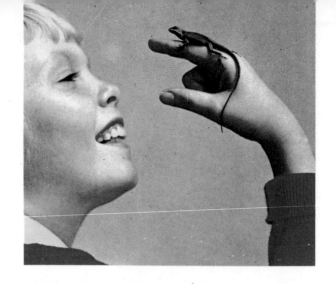

Lizards

IN appearance and habit, lizards are surprisingly like some of the ancient dinosaurs. They are not direct descendants of those extinct reptiles, but they do belong to the same broad family. A pair of lizards in a terrarium can give you a miniature picture of what life could have been like millions of years ago during the age of dinosaurs.

Most of our lizards are found in the desert and semi-desert areas of the west and southwest. They are creatures that like a dry and sunny climate. A few fence lizards range along the eastern coast as far north as Maryland and New Jersey. The American chameleon and the skink are also eastern lizards, but they are found mostly in the woodlands of the south.

All lizards have dry, scaly skin and lidded eyes. While salamanders are semi-aquatic, lizards prefer to live on dry land.

Most lizards make good pets if you take the trouble to house and feed them properly. A desert terrarium like the one described on page 46 usually makes an ideal home. American chameleons and eastern fence lizards require a few more plants than their western relatives, but the basic set-up is essentially the same. Place the terrarium where the sun's rays can hit it, but be sure

Clark's spiny lizard, found among rocks and trees, is fast and hard to catch.

to provide shade also. If you keep the temperature at 70 degrees or above, your pets will always be active.

Lizards feed on all types of insects, and you will have to provide them with live flies, beetles, grasshoppers, and crickets to keep them healthy. This diet is not difficult to obtain during the summer. In wintertime, mealworms will serve as an adequate substitute.

A water dish buried in sand and surrounded by stones and scrubby plants can add to the attractiveness of your terrarium, but the chances are that your lizards won't drink from it. Most lizards get all the moisture they need from leaves and grass. An occasional light spraying of the plants in the terrarium will provide the necessary droplets.

Most lizards are quick-moving and difficult to catch, although the horned toad is a notable exception. If you grab an ordinary lizard by the tail, the tail is very likely to break off in your hand. Contrary to popular belief, a lizard's tail does not grow back completely.

Praying mantis

Insects

INSECTS are among nature's most plentiful creatures. They are easy to find and easy to care for. Space is no problem. You can keep a thriving insect zoo in a group of containers that will fit comfortably on a shelf or on top of a small table.

You can capture many interesting insects by "sweeping" through meadows with a large net.

During warm weather, almost any field, garden, lawn, or wood is a good spot to collect insects. Pick one such area and study it for a while. Watch the behavior of the various insects and decide which ones seem most interesting. Then you will be able to provide a suitable environment for the insects you capture.

You may notice, for example, that a caterpillar seems to prefer certain kinds of leaves. If you decide to make the caterpillar part of your collection, be sure to bring back some of the leaves also.

You can re-create the natural surroundings of many insects in as simple a container as a glass jar or a bowl. A small aquarium, terrarium, or home-made glass box can be used for more elaborate displays.

Daylight is important to the health of your insects, but do not expose them directly to the rays of the sun. The sun can quickly make an oven of any glass container.

Many insects are harmful to man, but the praying mantis is one of our best friends. It eats only other insects. A few praying mantises can keep a garden remarkably free of insect pests.

The "praying" in the mantis's name comes from the way it holds its forelegs together. It does indeed look as if it is praying, but any small insect which ventures close discovers too late that the mantis assumes this

A fruit jar with a wire mesh cover is
a fine home for most insects.

position to enable it to spring on its prey.

Specimens may be found in many gardens, or in patches of overgrown grass. A praying mantis should be housed in a well-planted wire-mesh cage or glass container. You must keep it supplied with beetles, flies, and other easily obtainable insects. Do not put two adult mantises in the same cage, because one will probably kill and eat the other.

All insects go through some kind of transformation as they develop, but the change from caterpillar to cocoon to butterfly or moth is one of the most spectacular.

You will be able to watch this entire process if you bring home a caterpillar and surround it with its favorite leaves and twigs. The caterpillar is the larva of the butterfly or moth. When it spins itself into a cocoon, it goes into the pupa stage. If you find a cocoon on a twig, you can snip off the entire twig and bring it home to plant in your cage, which should be kept quite moist. One day a beautiful butterfly or moth will push its way out of the cocoon and hang head down from the twig for a while until it gathers the strength to fly. At this time you should release it, for it cannot live in a small enclosure.

There are many other insects which are easy to keep and fascinating to observe. Among these interesting insects are walking sticks, katydids, and dragon flies.

Health and First Aid

UNUSUAL behavior in any animal should alert you to the possibility that it is sick or has been injured. The characteristic signs are sluggishness, loss of weight or other changes in appearance, and refusal to eat. However, an animal in pain may also become exceptionally active, rushing around its cage or biting at the affected part of its body.

You must be particularly careful about handling an animal at such times. A wild animal's instinct is to hide itself when it is not feeling well, and you may frighten or anger it if you pick it up suddenly. A pet skunk, raccoon, or flying squirrel should be handled with gloves when it seems to be in poor health.

If a preliminary examination does not reveal an obvious source of the trouble—a wound, a broken bone, inflamed skin or eyes, or parasitic insects such as lice—you may have to depend on nature to effect a cure. You can help things along by making sure that the cage is clean, that fresh food

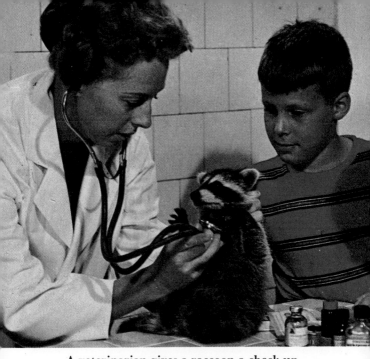

A veterinarian gives a raccoon a check-up.

and water are constantly available, and that a comfortable temperature is maintained at all times. If you have more than one pet, keep the sick animal in isolation to avoid infecting others.

It is wise to obtain the advice of an expert whenever you can. If you bought your pet from a local dealer, you might ask him for suggestions. Be sure to describe the symptoms accurately. He may recognize the disease as one to which the animal is particularly susceptible, and for which there is a simple remedy.

The person best able to treat your sick pet, of course, is a veterinarian. He or she should be consulted if the animal shows no signs of recovery, or for serious injuries such as broken limbs or wings. Use a cage to take the animal to the veterinarian's office, and make sure that it is protected from drafts and sudden changes in temperature.

You can keep illness to a minimum by providing your wildlife pets with clean surroundings, adequate exercise, and a properly balanced diet.

Mammal and bird cages should be cleaned every day. Water in tanks and terrariums should not be allowed to become foul. Moist areas in woodland and semi-aquatic terrariums must be checked frequently for mildew.

Adding vitamins and cod liver oil to your pets' diet helps to keep them in good health. This is particularly important with small active mammals which may not get all the exercise they normally require.

The claws of mammals and the beaks of

some birds must be filed down regularly. In the wild, this is taken care of by the animal's search for food, but it must be done for them in captivity. The first time that clipping is required, take the animal to the veterinarian and watch carefully how it is done. If you are careful enough, you may be able to do the job next time yourself, or one of your parents can do it for you.

Birds and mammals are also subject to attacks of lice and other insect pests. These can be treated with any of the pest-killing powders on the market. Remove your pet to a clean, temporary cage and dust its coat or feathers liberally. Be sure to clean and disinfect the old cage before you return the animal to it.

Mange, a skin disease attacking fur-bearing mammals, may also be treated at home. Ask your pet dealer for an effective remedy and follow the directions carefully.

Cuts and open wounds should be cleaned gently with a 70% solution of alcohol. If a bandage is required, tie gauze around the injured part, but never use adhesive tape.

Shopping for Pets

A good pet dealer can supply most any animal you want from his store or by mail. But, before you decide to buy a pet, be sure that you can give it a suitable home, and that you are prepared to take proper care of it.

Once you have decided upon the pet you want to buy, inspect it carefully to make e that it is in good health and has a dly disposition. It is always a good idea to take a newly purchased pet to a veterinarian or zoo for a check-up. This is particularly wise in the case of animals that arrive by mail. Even if the pet was in good condition when it was shipped, it may have been subjected to extremes of temperature or caught some disease when traveling. By having it examined, you avoid the possibility of infecting other pets, as well as the unhappy experience of caring for a sick or dying pet.

If your local dealer is unable to provide you with the particular pet you want, he may be able to recommend a reputable

Ground uta

Spotted turtle

mail order firm. Before you place any order, however, be sure to check with your local game warden or the officials of your state's fish and game agency. It is against the law in some states to keep certain animals. You can save yourself a great deal of trouble by checking in advance.

The cost of various animals changes slightly from year to year. The following list will, however, give you an idea of how much some of the more popular pets may cost.

PET	PRICE RANGE
Skunk	$ 40 to 45
Raccoon	20 to 40
Crow or magpie	30 to 35
Turtle	1 to 2
Frog or toad	.50 to 1.00
Salamander	.25 to 1.00
Lizard	.50 to 1.50
Field Mouse	.50 to 1.00

There will be regional differences depending on the availability of the animal.

INDEX

ASPCA, 8
Amphibians, 10, 53

Bait, 11-12, 37
Beaks, care of, 74-75
Beetle, 70
Bullfrog, 60
Butterfly, 71

Cages, 19-25
Caterpillar, 71
Chameleon, 65
Chipmunk, 13
Claws, care of, 74-75
Clipping, wings, 40
Cocoon, 71
Crows, 39-42
Cuts, 75

Deer mouse, 36
Disinfectant, 25
Dragon fly, 71

Exercise wheel, 36

Fence lizard, 64
Field mice, 36-38
First aid, 75
Flies, 70
Flying squirrel, 72
Frogs, 53-60

Handling, 17
Havahart trap, 12
Hibernation, 29, 34-35, 49
Horned toad, 66

Illness and injury, 72-75
Insects, 67-71

Katydid, 71

Leopard frog, 56
Lice, 75
Live-catch trap, 11
Lizards, 10, 46, 64-66

Magpie, 42
Mail order firms, 78
Mange, 75
Metabolism wheel, 37
Mice, 11, 16, 36-38
Moth, 71

Nesting box, 23
Newt, 63

Pet dealers, 73, 76
Praying mantis, 69-71

Raccoons, 11, 16, 32-35
Reptiles, 10

Salamanders, 61-63
Skunks, 16, 27-31, 72
Spiny lizard, 65
Spotted salamander, 62, 63
Snapping turtle, 52
Squirrels, 15

Tadpoles, 54-55
Terrariums, 15, 43-46
Toads, 53-60
Trapping, 7-13
Turtles, 47-52
Turtles, soft shells, 52

Veterinarian, 13, 74, 77
Vitamins, 51, 74

Walking stick, 71
White footed mouse, 36

Zoos, 18